CONTENTS

GU00832083

THE NATIONALISED INDUSTRIES

I.—INTRODUCTION

1. This White Paper replies to the recommendations in the report of November 1976 by the National Economic Development Office, "A study of U.K. Nationalised Industries: their role in the economy and control in the future." It takes into account the Government's plans for developing industrial democracy in the nationalised industries, and it explains the Government's main proposals in response to the report of August 1976 by the National Consumer Council on "Consumers and the Nationalised Industries".

2. The White Paper is about the control of the nationalised industries, their financial and economic objectives, and their relations with government. It sets out proposals designed to reconcile the purposes of public ownership with the independence needed for vigorous and enterprising management; and to ensure that the nationalised industries employ resources efficiently to the benefit of the whole community. Section II describes a number of institutional changes intended to improve the relationship between the nationalised industries and government, unions, customers and suppliers. It explains how information on the industries' main objectives, agreed after discussion between the Government and the boards, and on their performance will be published. Section III discusses the financial and economic framework within which the industries will operate, and in particular the role of the financial targets which will be published for all the industries and used as a measure of their success.

3. The central problem in evolving an acceptable relationship between the Government and the nationalised industries has always been how best to reconcile the boards' need for sufficient freedom to manage the industries with the Government's legitimate interests in them. The Government must be concerned in the strategies, and operational decisions of public importance, of industries which are basic to the national economy; in seeing that these industries, which are not subject to the private sector discipline of the threat of bankruptcy, and are in some cases relatively free from market pressures, are efficient; and in ensuring that there is an acceptable return on the public capital invested in them.

4. The last general review of the economic and financial principles common to all nationalised industries was the White Paper of 1967, "Nationalised Industries: a review of economic and financial objectives", Cmnd. 3437. That White Paper was intended to show how investment, pricing and efficiency policies would be taken into account in setting financial objectives, rather than to make any change in the basic relationship between the Government and the nationalised industries. It explained that, subject to allowance where necessary for social objectives or for meeting statutory obligations, it was the Government's policy to treat the nationalised industries as commercial bodies so far as the expected return on investment was concerned. It set out criteria for investment appraisal and pricing policy, which were intended to ensure that the nationalised industries did not claim resources which could have been put to better use in other parts of the economy. It stressed the importance of setting

the industries clear financial targets which would serve both as an incentive to management and as one of the standards by which success or failure would be judged.

5. These principles were endorsed by the Select Committee on Nationalised Industries and generally accepted as setting a sound basis for future relations and control. In practice, however, the new approach did not last, and in the first half of the 1970's the relations between governments and the industries deteriorated. This arose in part because of disagreements and uncertainty over the plans of particular industries. But, the main single factor which undermined the principles in the 1967 White Paper was the price restraint policies of the early 1970's. The Post Office and the gas and electricity industries were forced into deficit and for the first time ever had to be subsidised to cover their losses, which totalled £1,182 million over the period. The grants which were already being paid to British Rail escalated as their fares and charges were held down and their deficit increased. As a result of these policies, the financial targets of most of the nationalised industries had to be abandoned and there was little chance to put the 1967 principles to the test.

6. In its report of December 1973, "Capital Investment Procedures" (H.C. 1973–74, 65), the S.C.N.I. concluded that government had failed to meet its objective "of exercising its control publicly and according to well-defined ground rules, without interfering with the management functions of the industries themselves". The Committee accordingly recommended that the Government should arrange for "a detailed study of the role of the nationalised industries in the economy and of the way in which they are to be controlled in the future".

7. In June 1975, in its reply to the S.C.N.I.'s report, the Government announced that it had asked the N.E.D.O. to undertake this enquiry. The N.E.D.O. published their report on 18th November, 1976. It is a searching and highly critical examination of the relations between the industries and governments. In his introduction to the report, the Director General of the N.E.D.O. wrote:—

"Our enquiry has left us in no doubt that the existing framework of relationships, developed under governments of both main political parties, is unsatisfactory and in need of radical change".

8. Many of the industries, in their written evidence to the Select Committee on Nationalised Industries,* generally agree with the N.E.D.O.'s analysis of the problems. Some, however, comment that their relations with their sponsoring departments have always been generally good and others agree that they have recently improved. Indeed the N.E.D.O. acknowledge that their criticisms do not apply to relationships with all the nationalised industries or for all the time to particular industries. The Government agrees, nevertheless, with their general conclusion that relations had deteriorated in the period up to the mid-1970's and needed to be improved. The N.E.D.O. present a perceptive and thoughtful analysis of the problems and, while the Government does not accept all their proposals, it welcomes their report as offering a basis on which both the Government and the industries can now build.

---

*Published by the S.C.N.I. in their Second Special Report of 1976–77 (H.C. 345), "Comments by Nationalised Industries on the N.E.D.O. Report".

The Government's general approach

9. In 1974 the Government set out to put the nationalised industries back on to a sound economic and financial footing. This required substantial price increases to phase out the subsidies necessitated by price restraint, described in paragraph 5 above. As a result, the industries are generally in a much stronger financial position than they have been for a number of years. The period of rapid price increases needed to deal with the deficits due to price restraint in the early 1970s is over. A more stable, and better, climate of relationship has been established and it is, therefore, now timely to review, and where necessary develop, the principles in the 1967 White Paper. The Government considers that this review, together with the other measures discussed in this White Paper, will lay the foundations for further improvement.

10. An important point which must be emphasised from the beginning is that apart from the fact of public ownership and control many of the nationalised industries have little in common. They vary in size, objectives, competitive position, markets, financial strength, and social significance. The individual energy and transport industries are subject to overall policies for the sectors in which they operate. The formation of the two new manufacturing corporations, British Aerospace and British Shipbuilders, brings about a further significant shift in the balance of the nationalised industries away from the historical pre-dominance of the public utilities serving a British market. The three manu-facturing industries—Steel, Aerospace and Shipbuilding—together with British Airways and the British National Oil Corporation all operate in highly com-petitive international markets with their prices largely set by international trading conditions. It is important that these industries, and indeed those which are competing in domestic markets, are able to respond quickly to opportunities and competitive forces and that the Government's arrangements with them should recognise this. It follows that, while there are a number of important principles of wide application, it is essential throughout to take account of the varying circumstances of the different industries and to be ready to find solutions and a framework of control appropriate to the particular needs and market situations of each of them. This need for a flexible approach to match circumstances is recognised by the N.E.D.O.

11. The N.E.D.O. discuss in some detail the crucial question whether the Government should aim to stand back from the industries, and operate an "arms-length" relationship, or whether it should be involved more closely. Their conclusions on this are worth quoting:—

"It seems to us that the thinking behind the wholly arm's length approach is based on a false analogy with the private sector. The financial structures and disciplines in the public and private sectors are very different—not least because the ultimate sanction of liquidation is in practice absent in the major nationalised industries. Moreover, their importance as employers, suppliers and customers, and the economic and social implications of their actions make it right as well as inevitable that government should take a close interest in their strategies. The issues of public policy involved are so large and politically sensitive that it is not realistic to suppose that they would ever be left for long to management alone to determine, subject only to periodic checks on their financial performance."

7

The Government agrees with this. The question is how best to construct with each industry a relationship which is sufficiently close, but in which the responsibilities and objectives of both the Government and the industry are well defined and well understood.

II.—INSTITUTIONAL PROPOSALS

Board structure

12. The N.E.D.O. recommend a radical change in the current institutional arrangements. As a general approach, but with modifications to suit circumstances, they propose that each nationalised industry should be run by a Policy Council responsible for strategy and a Corporation Board acting as the executive authority. The Policy Council would be under a President of high personal standing, and preferably a part-timer. It would include the Chairman and some members of the Corporation Board, representatives of the main interest groups concerned with the industry—government departments, trade unions, and customers—and also members reflecting other independent viewpoints. It would be supported by a small staff seconded from departments, the Corporation and trade unions. Its main functions would be to agree corporate objectives and the strategies to achieve them; to establish performance criteria; to endorse corporate plans; and to monitor performance.

13. The Corporation Board would manage the industry within the framework of these objectives, strategies and criteria. One of the main roles of the President of the Policy Council would be to protect the Corporation Board, which would have a separate Chairman, from intervention by government in carrying out its responsibilities. The Policy Council would appoint the Chairman and members of the Board.

14. The Government agrees that, in dealing with the nationalised industries, its main concern should be with strategic and major issues rather than with day to day management. It also generally accepts N.E.D.O.'s argument that the evolution of strategic plans for nationalised industries should be a combined operation, involving consultation between the interest groups which are closely concerned with their content and implementation and which often have the power to frustrate them if they wish. However, the Government does not accept that N.E.D.O.'s proposal for Policy Councils and Corporation Boards is the best way of achieving these objectives and of improving its relations with the industries.

15. Before reaching this conclusion the Government discussed the proposal with the nationalised industries, and took account of the comments in their published evidence to the S.C.N.I. None of the industries favours—and some reject in very strong terms—the proposal for a Policy Council standing in line of command between the Minister and an executive Board which runs the industry. They assume that Ministers would not delegate their present powers, or concern with matters of major importance, to the Policy Council (and this appears to be implicit in the N.E.D.O.'s proposal if it were to achieve the desired objective of limiting ministerial intervention). This assumption is right. The Government is the sole shareholder of the nationalised industries, and their principal banker; and, as the N.E.D.O. acknowledge, the industries' strategies and main policy decisions involve questions of major political and public importance with which the Government must be concerned.

16. The Government believes that, contrary to the N.E.D.O.'s objectives, these arrangements would slow down the process of decision making and would confuse responsibility and accountability. The Minister and the Policy

Council would both be concerned with strategic and major issues. The functions of the Policy Council and the Corporation Board, each with a statutory role, would overlap because, as many of the industries have pointed out, the distinction between strategic and executive decisions is not in practice always as sharp and as clear cut as N.E.D.O.'s proposals imply. Thus, the Government, the Policy Council and the Corporation Board could all be concerned with strategic and major issues, and instead of clarifying responsibilities and streamlining decisions, the N.E.D.O.'s proposals would add an additional layer of authority, expressed in legislation, in a Policy Council whose own responsibilities would in practice have unclear demarcation lines.

17. A number of the nationalised industries have also pointed out that their present boards are supported by management committees which deal with many of the day to day issues involved in the running of the business. These arrangements are flexible and tailored to the requirements of the particular industry whose Chairman or board can readily modify them if necessary. They are, however, fundamentally different from a statutory two tier structure, with the powers and functions of the senior board "explicitly and formally distinguished from those of executive management", as proposed by N.E.D.O.

18. In their paper of November 1977, to the S.C.N.I.*, the N.E.D.O. have criticised the industries' reactions to their proposals for Policy Councils and Corporation Boards. They argue that it is unacceptable for the industries to agree generally with their analysis of the failings of the arrangements in the past but to reject any proposals for structural or other changes to ensure a better and more stable relationship in future. While the Government recognises the deficiencies which led the N.E.D.O. to make their recommendations, many have been overcome since N.E.D.O. conducted their study and the Government does not agree that it follows that major structural changes in the boards are a necessary condition of maintaining the recent improvement in relationships.

19. The fact that the Government does not intend to introduce Policy Councils and Corporation Boards does not mean, however, that it rejects the argument that changes are necessary to bring about further improvements. The Government is already developing a number of new arrangements on the lines proposed by N.E.D.O., and it will now introduce others. Later parts of this section explain the various ways in which the main interest groups concerned with the industries will be more involved in the formulation of their policies, either by board membership or by improved consultative and participative arrangements. The procedures for the discussion of corporate plans are being developed with the aim of giving them a central place in the relationship between the nationalised industries and the sponsoring departments, and of providing a systematic framework for reaching agreement on long-term objectives and strategies. Information on these plans, on financial targets and any sectoral or social objectives set to the industries, on cash limits, and on performance and service indicators and aims will be published in the industries' annual reports and accounts. These arrangements, and the proposed new power to give specific directions where necessary, will help to clarify the respective roles of the boards and of the Government, and they will provide a better basis for Parliament and the public to judge the performance of the industries and the role of the Government in their operations.

*Published by the SCNI in their Second Special Report of 1977–78 (HC 28).

New powers to issue specific directions to boards

20. The present statutes empower the Secretary of State to give the boards directions of "a general character" on matters which appear to him to affect the national interest and, in some cases, directions on particular subjects which are specified in the statutes. However, the power to give general directions does not allow the Secretary of State to direct an individual industry on a particular matter, however important, unless that particular power of direction is specified in the statutes. In the absence of powers to give specific directions, governments have had to rely on a process of persuasion. Because this has been informal, accountability for decisions has on occasions been blurred and this has caused friction and resentment. The Government considers that this situation should be avoided, and that it is wrong in principle that a Minister cannot statutorily intervene in specific matters of major importance subject to the approval of Parliament. It agrees, therefore, with N.E.D.O. that the present powers should be extended to remedy this deficiency by enabling the Minister to give a board either general or specific directions on matters which appeared to him to affect the national interest. An important advantage of the new power would be that when a direction was given it would clarify accountability by indicating formally and publicly where the Government had decided to overrule a board's judgment or to direct it to do something in the national interest. The Government will put forward proposals accordingly for amendment of the statutes.

21. These legislative proposals will include a number of safeguards. A Minister would not be able to issue a specific direction before he has consulted the industry in question. The direction would be in the form of a statutory instrument, subject to Parliamentary procedures. The Minister would be required to publish, when the statutory instrument was presented, an estimate of the extra cost if any to the industry of implementing the direction. If the industry did not agree with this, their estimate would be published with the Government's comments on it. Compensation would be paid where appropriate to cover the extra cost and the legislation would provide for this. There would also be powers to override, where necessary and subject to European Community obligations, any other duties except financial duties laid on an industry by its statutes, where the specific direction might conflict with these. It would not be possible to make a specific direction which would have the effect of extending or restricting the existing statutory powers of an industry; that would be a matter for new primary legislation.

22. If Parliament approves these powers the Government intends to use them sparingly. One of the themes running through this White Paper is that the relationship between governments and nationalised industries is close; and there will continue to be many issues on which the industries and the Government will reach agreement without the issue of specific directions and without any confusion of responsibility or accountability. Moreover, Ministers do not intend that, as a result of the availability of this power, they should be drawn into detailed intervention or Parliamentary discussion of a multitude of matters of day to day management, which should in principle, and must in practice, be left to those responsible for managing and running these industries without the intervention of Ministers or Parliament.

Pay and appointment of board members

23. When the Review Body on Top Salaries in their Sixth Report recommended revised salaries for nationalised industry board members and Chairmen for 1st January 1975, the Government deferred a decision on the recommendations for wider policy reasons. As a result the pay of board members and Chairmen has fallen sharply in real terms, far more so relatively than that of most other people, and there are anomalies in the pay structure in many of the industries with board members earning less than some senior staff working for them.

24. On 15th December the Government announced that the most that could be allowed at the present time was a 5% general increase from 1st January, 1978, with up to 10% for the less well paid board members tapered to ensure that the 5% applied above £13,000 a year. In reaching this decision the Government had regard to the measures still being taken in the national interest to control inflation which continue to demand considerable restraint from all sections of the community. The Government recognised that this still leaves nationalised industry board members significantly out of line with their counterparts, and it will look again at the way forward when the Review Body on Top Salaries makes its next recommendations for April 1978.

25. All appointments to boards will continue to be made by the responsible Minister who will consult the Chairman of the industry concerned on each appointment, and call on the Public Appointments Unit in the Civil Service Department when appropriate. A number of the industries have been critical of delays in filling vacancies on the boards. This is sometimes unavoidable but the Government readily accepts that the aim must be to avoid delays wherever possible.

The composition of boards

26. The composition of each board will be settled on an industry by industry basis by the Ministers concerned after discussion with the Chairmen. The Government's plans for the appointment of employee representatives are explained in paragraph 28 on industrial democracy; and, as pointed out in paragraph 30, consumer members will be appointed to some boards. The Government will continue to appoint part-time non-executive members who are not representative of interest groups but who have the experience to make an important contribution to the running of the industries.

27. The Government has also decided that in some industries a civil servant from the sponsoring department, and in a few cases from the Treasury too, will be appointed to boards after consultation with the Chairmen concerned. The purpose is to give the department a clearer understanding of the industry, and a better insight into its problems, but the Government also recognises that in the different circumstances of the various industries appointment of civil servants to the boards will not necessarily be the best way of securing this result in every industry. It will, however, be worthwhile where it means that the Government can be aware at an earlier stage than now of the thinking of the boards and, for their part, the boards can have a clearer view, at a formative stage of their planning, of the wider objectives and implications of Government policy. There is a potential difficulty arising from the dual allegiance which a civil servant would have to his Minister on the one hand and as a board member

sharing the corporate responsibility of the board on the other hand. So long as this duality does not in practice produce irreconcilable conflict, it presents no obstacle to adopting the arrangement. There are already civil servants on the boards of the British National Oil Corporation and of the Atomic Energy Authority. This has worked well and their presence has proved useful both for the Government and for the two Corporations. The practical course is to experiment with the arrangement in other cases also where it is expected to be helpful.

Industrial democracy

28. Management and the unions in the nationalised industries are already making progress in developing new arrangements for consultation and participation. In the Post Office they have agreed on an experiment, lasting for two years, for a new board with, in addition to the Chairman, seven management and seven union Members, and five independent Members. In some of the other industries, the management and the unions have chosen to put the emphasis on the improvement of their existing consultative procedures rather than on involvement at board level. The Government welcomes these initiatives, and intends to encourage progress in introducing and improving schemes of industrial democracy at all levels in the nationalised industries. It has accordingly asked the Chairmen of the nationalised industries to consult with the unions in each industry, where they are not already doing so, and to make joint proposals for further improvements in consultation and participation. The Government has asked the Chairmen to put forward their proposals by August 1978. They might range from worker representation at board and lower levels to further developments in consultative and participative procedures. It is likely that any proposals which emerge can go ahead quickly under present legislation. However, if in any nationalised industries it is necessary to amend the statutes to allow for an experiment, or for new arrangements, the Government will introduce the necessary legislation, as it did for the Post Office experiment.

29. The Government will publish a White Paper on its views on the way forward in industrial democracy in the private sector as well as the nationalised industries.

Consumers

30. In April 1975 the Government asked the National Consumer Council (N.C.C.) to review the arrangements for consumer representation in the nationalised industries. The recommendations in the N.C.C.'s thorough and detailed report* were not concerned with the manufacturing industries such as the British Steel Corporation but only with those industries which impinge directly on the domestic consumer. It was published in August 1976 and the Government has had wide-ranging consultations on its recommendations, some of which it has already implemented. The Government sees an important continuing role for the nationalised industry consumer councils as spokesmen and guardians of the consumer interest, working in close association with the N.C.C. at national level, and with local authority and other advisory services at local level. It also sees a role for consumer members on some nationalised industry boards.

---

*Consumers and the nationalised industries, Report by National Consumer Council to the Secretary of State for Prices and Consumer Protection. H.M.S.O.

Powers of consumer councils

31. The N.C.C. were concerned that nationalised industries should give more weight to the views of their consumer councils, and recommended in particular that the Government should have a power to issue directions to an industry following consumer council recommendations; such powers already exist in respect of several of the nationalised industries concerned but there are some important exceptions. For the most part, normal relations between consumer councils and their industries will make Government intervention of this kind unnecessary. In most cases in which a consumer council makes a recommendation, the industry and council should be able to reach agreement between themselves on the necessary action. The same will be true also of discussions on the amount of information which the industries should disclose to the councils and the minimum period of notice which they should give to them before implementing the major proposals. In cases of disagreement it would be open to a consumer council to make representations to the Government, which would decide whether to give the industry a specific direction, using, where necessary, the new powers discussed in paragraphs 20–22 above, and subject, as noted there, to any conflict with our European Community obligations. The N.C.C. has also proposed that, whenever an industry failed to act on a recommendation from its consumer council the Secretary of State should be required to issue a direction unless both Houses of Parliament, by Order, specifically agreed that he should not. The Government does not accept this view: it considers that existing procedures are adequate to ensure that Parliament has an opportunity to challenge Ministerial decisions. The Government, however, welcomes the proposal that research reports by the councils should be available to the Select Committee on Nationalised Industries, and notes that the Select Committee already receives evidence from them.

Energy

32. In the light of the recommendations of the N.C.C. and of the Plowden Committee*, the Government has established an Electricity Consumers' Council (E.C.C.) for England and Wales, initially on a non-statutory basis. The Council will fill an important gap in previous arrangements by giving English and Welsh electricity consumers an effective voice at national, as well as regional, level, where it will operate alongside the National Gas and Domestic Coal Consumers' Councils. The Government intends to introduce legislation to make the E.C.C. statutory and to give it responsibility for co-ordinating regional electricity consumer representation. The National Gas Consumers' Council (N.G.C.C.) will continue to guide and co-ordinate the activities of the regional councils to ensure that gas consumers' views are given coherent and authoritative expression. The Government also intends to introduce legislation giving the Domestic Coal Consumers' Council a statutory right to be informed by the National Coal Board of its plans, arrangements and proposals and imposing a duty on the Board to consider any representations made by the Council.

33. Consumer Advice Centres and Citizens' Advice Bureaux already deal with large numbers of enquiries and complaints about public sector goods

---

*The Structure of the Electricity Supply Industry in England and Wales, Report by Committee of Enquiry to the Secretary of State for Energy: Cmnd. 6398.

and services generally and the Government agrees with the N.C.C. that they are an easily identified and convenient source of advice and help for consumers with problems of this kind including domestic fuel problems. However, the Government believes that the regional gas and area electricity consumers' and consultative councils, with their district committees, should continue to play a valuable role as specialists in addition to the generalist agencies, as well as feeding in consumers' views to the national bodies. Over 2,000 experienced men and women give their time voluntarily in this work and are available with advice and assistance to the public outside normal hours; they play an important part in advising local nationalised industry management and monitoring their performance, and provide the grassroots contact for formulating a consumer view at national level. The Government proposes to continue its support for these bodies, but will have further discussions with the E.C.C. and N.G.C.C. and those responsible for the local authority and other generalist services with a view to ensuring the most efficient liaison and integration between the various advice agencies.

34. The newly established Energy Commission, on which domestic and industrial consumers are represented, will provide a valuable forum in which a consumer view can be brought to bear at the highest level. The Government has asked the N.C.C. to give the three energy consumer council representatives its support in co-ordinating the views of consumer and voluntary organisations and providing research and secretarial services.

Surface transport

35. The Government intends in due course to promote legislation to extend the powers of the existing Central Transport Consultative Committee, at present prescribed by Section 56 of the Transport Act 1962. It will be renamed the National Transport Consumers' Council (N.T.C.C.), and enabled to consider the general tariff structure of the British Railways Board's railway passenger and parcels services; to consider a wide range of services and facilities provided by other transport operators, including bus services; and to make appropriate representations to the operators, the Traffic Commissioners or the Price Commission, as the case may be.

36. The Government believes, however, that it would be inappropriate for complaints about individual bus services to be handled by a national body. Furthermore the proposed introduction of Public Transport Plans will place upon shire counties in England and Wales additional responsibilities in the planning of bus services. In these circumstances the Government takes the view that county councils should set up, under their general powers, advisory committees with representatives of consumer interests as well as council members. These advisory committees, which might be modelled upon the Transport Users' Advisory Committees already in existence in Passenger Transport Authority areas, would assist the county councils in their preparation of Public Transport Plans, deal with complaints about bus services in their area and co-operate with local generalist advice services. They will report to the local authority who would, under existing powers, be competent to make representations to the Traffic Commissioners as appropriate. The local authorities, the new advisory committees and the existing area Transport Users' Consultative Committees (T.U.C.C.s) would be expected to establish

liaison on matters of common interest.   The remit of such advisory committees, as of the T.U.C.C.s, may later need to be reviewed in the light of Government decisions following consultations on the issues relating to local railway services that are particularly cost-ineffective, as set out in paragraphs 98–105 of the White Paper on Transport Policy (Cmnd. 6836).

Posts and telecommunications

37. The Government will give careful consideration to the recommendations of the Post Office Review Committee* relating to consumer representation. In the meantime, it has decided as part of the two year experiment in industrial democracy in the Post Office that there should be two members with experience of consumer affairs on the Post Office Board, appointed after consultation with the Secretary of State for Prices and Consumer Protection.

Aviation

38. The Civil Aviation Authority, which is responsible for the Airline Users' Committee, has given the Committee new terms of reference which ensure that it has a clearly autonomous position with an independent Chairman and secretariat, a more positive role in furthering the interests of air transport users and a responsibility to co-operate with the airport consultative committees.

Scotland, Wales and Northern Ireland

39. For those nationalised industries which operate on a United Kingdom basis, the arrangements described will also apply in Scotland, Wales and Northern Ireland, with minor variations, though account will be taken of the particular need to provide for the consideration of national issues of special concern to each of those countries.   In Scotland, however, the electricity and bus industries need separate arrangements. The two Scottish Electricity Consultative Councils will remain, with their joint Secretariat, responsible to the Secretary of State for Scotland, as recommended by the Scottish Consumer Council.   The Secretary of State for Scotland is consulting local authority, transport and consumer interests about the possible adoption in Scotland of consumer representation arrangements similar to those proposed for the bus industries in England and Wales.   The Government will take account of the views expressed in deciding whether or not new arrangements should be made. In Northern Ireland, the Electricity Consumers' Council, and the Transport Users' Committee (which deals with bus, rail and airport facilities) will continue to represent their particular consumer interests, with liaison as appropriate with other consumer bodies in the United Kingdom.

Other consultative arrangements

40. In addition to the proposals discussed so far, the Government is developing other ways of involving the main interest groups in the forward planning of an industry or a sector.   Since 1974 the main policy questions in the coal industry have been discussed on a tripartite basis between the Government, the Coal Board and the coal unions.   Last year the Secretary of State for Energy appointed an Energy Commission which will advise him on the development

*Report of the Post Office Review Committee to the Secretary of State for Industry, Cmnd. 6850.

of an energy strategy for the United Kingdom and on other energy policy issues. The Commission includes representatives of the energy industries and trade unions, and industrial, consumer and other interests. The recent White Paper on Transport Policy, Cmnd. 6836, considered a number of ways in which the Government wanted to see consultation on the formulation and execution of transport policy improved, both at the local level and nationally. In addition, the Government is exploring further with the N.E.D.O. and with both sides of industry its ideas of setting up an Economic Development Committee for transport as one means of promoting, in the context of the industrial strategy, the regular consultation between the Government, management and the unions on plans for transport.

Relations with suppliers

41. The N.E.D.O. point out that the nationalised industries' technical dominance and the scale of their purchases means that certain supplying industries have become almost wholly dependent on their strategic decisions and related investment programmes. Because of this several important studies have been commissioned by the National Economic Development Council since 1975 on various aspects of the relationship between the industries and their suppliers. This relationship is generally close, and given the strong bond of common interest between the two, the Government attaches a good deal of importance to this. A number of ideas and improvements were discussed in a N.E.D.O. report in 1975, and the involvement of the nationalised industries in the Economic Development Committees and associated N.E.D.O. working parties and industrial strategy sector groups gives both the industries and their suppliers a forum for tackling further questions of common interest.

42. There is also considerable scope for the nationalised industries and their suppliers to co-operate in export promotion to their mutual benefit. The N.E.D.O. studies of this include examinations of the technical specifications laid down by the nationalised industries, with a view to aligning them where possible with international requirements so as to give the supplying industries a better chance of securing export orders; and also the promotion of co-operation between nationalised and private industry to allow them to compete together for major overseas projects, such as steelworks and railway construction and modernisation. In 1976, the nationalised industries set up special arrangements to promote collaboration between themselves and their customers and suppliers in the pursuit and development of exports. In addition, there are growing opportunities for sales of hardware and equipment by nationalised industries acting on their own account, or in participation with the private sector. The Government strongly welcomes all these initiatives and the positive role which the nationalised industries are taking, both jointly with the private sector and also on their own behalf in selling consultancy services to overseas countries and developing export opportunities generally.

Corporate plans and investment and financing reviews

43. For many years the development plans and investment programmes of the nationalised industries, covering periods of 5 years ahead, have increasingly been formulated within the wider context of both the industries' and the Government's objectives and policies. This process of corporate planning, covering various time periods, involves a continuing dialogue on long-term strategy,

medium-term development plans, and annual operating plans and budgets. The industries look to the Government for guidance on industrial policies, on economic prospects, and where appropriate on sectoral policies, including the social objectives underlying the payment of grant from public funds. The Government looks to the industries for data on markets, supplies and production. The development of this process is more advanced with some of the industries than others. Its benefits are already becoming apparent in the energy sector where over the past year or so a joint Working Group on Energy Strategy (with membership drawn at board level from the nationalised industries and from government departments) has contributed materially to the harmonization of planning timetables and procedures, to the understanding of the industries' and Government's medium-term forecasting methods, and in particular to the joint examination of the implications of alternative energy sector strategies for the plans and prospects of the industries. The process of joint examination of issues affecting policies and plans is now to be carried further in the recently formed Energy Commission under the chairmanship of the Secretary of State for Energy. There have also been valuable developments in corporate planning in other nationalised industries, and the legislation establishing British Aerospace and British Shipbuilders requires the two Corporations in formulating their corporate plans to act on lines settled from time to time with the approval of the Secretary of State for Industry. The Railways Act 1974 made similar provision in relation to the Railways Board.

44. The Government considers that the corporate plan, and the examination of strategic options, should have a central place in the relationship between the nationalised industries and their sponsoring departments. As corporate planning is established more widely it will enable the annual review of the industries' medium-term investment programmes to take place in the context of known and understood longer term strategies. This is not to say that there will be no changes from year to year in the five year plans of the industries for implementing the agreed strategies. The industries regularly revise their five year programme, often substantially, to take account of changes in the outlook for the economy, in the demand for their particular products, in relative costs and prices, in the burden of their financing requirements, and in physical progress in the installation of new plants or of new buildings. Nationalised industries, like any commercial organisation, must continue to show flexibility and to make such changes. Moreover the strategic framework itself cannot be regarded as immutable. From time to time there are major long-term reviews of overall policy, covering either the whole future strategy of an industry or some crucial aspect of it, such as a technological decision on the choice of a new system. These represent an important turning point for an industry, and the Government accepts that, once long-term policy decisions are taken on this basis, they should not be reopened unless and until there has been a material change of circumstances. So that the Select Committee on Nationalised Industries, and the public, can be better informed of the industries' objectives the Government has asked them to publish in their annual reports and accounts a summary of the broad objectives in their corporate plan, and the main points in any major review, and any Government response to them.

45. The N.E.D.O. point out that the investment plans of a number of the nationalised industries have suffered over the years from intervention by

governments, through short-term cuts to reduce public expenditure or through intervention in previously agreed strategic plans. The dialogue between the Government and industries in the corporate planning process should help to provide a more stable framework. In addition the Government has made two changes in its procedures which it believes improve the way in which the industries' expenditure plans are handled and publicly presented.

46. Following an initiative in the N.E.D.C., in 1975, Ministers agreed that they would aim to give the industries by the end of the summer, rather than the end of the year, approval for 100% of their agreed investment programme for one year ahead, 85% for the second year and 70% for the third year (for which, under the previous procedures, no approval had been given at all). This new procedure helps the nationalised industries directly by enabling them to get on with implementing and rolling forward their plans. It also puts them in a position where they can help their supplying industries by drawing up firm plans earlier than had been possible hitherto.

47. The N.E.D.O. commented on the presentation of the nationalised industries' figures in statistics of public expenditure and the Government has made changes in line with their thinking. Under these new arrangements the investment programmes of the industries are still published in Public Expenditure White Papers, but it is the estimates of the funds to be provided towards this investment, in the form of loans, Public Dividend Capital or grants, which are included in the public expenditure totals. This new presentation recognises the essential difference between the nationalised industries, which finance a great deal of their investment from their earnings, and the generality of non-trading public services. The Government believes that it will also be helpful to the industries if on any future occasions it is necessary to involve them in any general exercise to reduce the planned level of public expenditure. Whereas previously any cuts they made had to be in their investment programmes, in future they will in principle be able as an alternative to take any other action which would reduce their requirements for external finance—such as cost savings and, subject to counter inflation policies, price increases. The presentation of these figures in the Public Expenditure White Paper shows loans and Public Dividend Capital, on which the industries are expected to pay interest and dividends, separately from grants given for social and regional purposes.

Monitoring

48. The N.E.D.O. consider that the boards are not effectively required to account for their performance in a systematic or objective manner. They point out that there is no external audit mechanism—additional to the present financial audit procedures—which might provide reassurance to Government and Parliament about the effectiveness of management organisation and procedures within the industries. They recommend that the annual report and accounts of each industry should in future include a statement of financial and other criteria and of achievement against them.

49. It is the responsibility of each board to monitor performance and efficiency within its industry but the Government agrees that it is also essential for the industries to account effectively to Parliament and to the public. It has, therefore, asked each of them to include in its annual report a statement

summarising and bringing together the Government's main current instru
tions and guidance, and also information on how it is measuring up to its
objectives.   There may be some information which an industry cannot publish
for reasons of commercial confidentiality.   But in general the statement would
include, for example, the main points in the corporate plan and any Government
response to them (see paragraph 44); the financial target, and the accompanying
Parliamentary statement explaining it, including any sectoral and social
objectives set for the industry (paragraph 73); the cash limit (paragraphs 79–82);
suitable aims in terms of performance and service (paragraph 78); and any
general or specific directions given to it (paragraph 20).   In its statement of how
well it was measuring up to these objectives, the industry would compare its
financial performance against its target and also its progress against its published
performance and service aims.   The systematic and regular publication of this
information will be an important development in response to the N.E.D.O.'s
report and one which will be helpful to the Select Committee on Nationalised
Industries, and to Parliament generally, in examining and monitoring the
performance of the industries, and of the departments which deal with them.
The Select Committee on Procedure is now conducting a major review of
Parliamentary procedure: if they make recommendations which have a bearing
on Parliament's relations with the nationalised industries these will be considered in addition to the arrangements described in this paragraph.

50. There are also a number of other ways in which the industries' activities
will come under independent scrutiny.   Under the Price Commission Act of
July 1977, the Price Commission has discretion, subject to Ministerial veto, to
investigate most price increases proposed by the nationalised industries.   (The
main exceptions are bus and air fares, which are controlled by the Traffic Commissioners and by the Civil Aviation Authority, and coal and most steel products
which are subject to European Coal and Steel Community regulations.)   If
Ministers direct it to do so, the Commission can also examine a nationalised
industry which is a monopoly supplier.   Secondly, the Government expects the
consumer councils to play an important role in monitoring the industries'
responsiveness to the needs of their customers and in making recommendations
on the services they give; and a number of ways in which the consumer council
arrangements have been strengthened are described in paragraphs 30–39.
Thirdly, the Government will be prepared on occasion to appoint special
committees of enquiry to examine the structure, performance and plans of
particular industries where it appears that there is a need for a far ranging
review.   The Government will keep under review the possibility of strengthening
arrangements for the external monitoring of those industries which enjoy
substantial protection from competition.

51. The Government also expects the industries to take the initiative in
strengthening their own systems for control and monitoring.   It therefore
welcomes the development of Audit Committees, which the National Coal
Board, the British Steel Corporation and a number of private sector companies
have recently been introducing, whereby a special group, usually including
part-time non-executive directors, examine and report on annual financial
statements, audit arrangements and internal financial controls.   The Government believes that this is a useful innovation which other nationalised industries
may wish to adopt.   It hopes that they will develop further the role of these

Audit Committees, or set up comparable arrangements, to look more generally at questions of efficiency and performance within their industry. The Government also expects that, in the normal exercise of their management functions, the industries will continue to take the initiative in calling in management consultants to undertake special studies when necessary.

III.—THE FINANCIAL AND ECONOMIC FRAMEWORK

General

52. The nationalised industries are major users of national resources. They employ about 1,700,000 people, or 7% of the country's total labour force. Their total investment this year and next is about £3,500 million at 1977 prices, and in 1976 they accounted for 14% of total fixed investment. A considerable part of their capital requirements is financed by advances from, or guaranteed by, the Government, and in 1976–77 these represented about 15% of the total Public Sector Borrowing Requirement of £8,800 million. In 1976 they contributed about 10% of the total output of the U.K. economy. They dominate four strategic sectors of economic activity: energy, public transport, communications and iron and steel. They supply basic goods and services to industry, and essentials of life to individual consumers. They are themselves major customers of some of the capital goods industries, and the scale of their purchases means that some of these supplying industries are heavily dependent on their strategic decisions and investment. In short, the nationalised industries have a pervasive influence throughout the economy on investment, employment, industrial costs, and on the cost of living. The share of national resources going to them, and the efficiency with which they use these resources, are matters of major importance.

53. This is why the Government has the responsibility to set out the broad financial and economic framework within which they want the industries to operate. The consequences of the price restraint policies of the early 1970s, and the suspension of financial targets and economic pricing policies over a wide area, illustrate the dangers of mismanaging this responsibility. For many nationalised industries this intervention led directly to mounting deficits financed by new and additional public expenditure on grants and loans which put other public sector priorities at risk; to indiscriminate subsidies from the taxpayer to the consumers; and in some cases to sharp reductions in investment and employment, affecting both the nationalised industries and their suppliers, when these policies had eventually to be reversed. As a result of this lack of direction, and its consequences, the morale of management and the workforce in the industries suffered badly.

54. It is essential that the mistakes of the early 1970s should not be repeated. The Government intends that the nationalised industries will not be forced into deficits by restraints on their prices. When help has to be given to poorer members of the community it will be given primarily through the social security and taxation systems and not by subsidising nationalised industry prices.

55. Now that the industries are generally in better shape, public attention—and sometimes criticism—is focussing on the size of their profits which result from the progressive return to economic pricing. However, although these reported profits may appear big when looked at in isolation they are by no means large when related to the net assets of the industries which are generating them. Indeed the real rates of return (that is, after allowing for inflation) being earned are still generally well below those in the private sector which themselves have been very low in recent years (see the chart on page 36, Appendix I). An adequate level of nationalised industry profits is essential to the continuing well being of the industries and their customers and of the economy as a whole.

They provide some of the funds for the very large investment programmes necessary to maintain supplies and services to the public. This keeps down the industries' new borrowing requirements, thus helping to reduce the burden of taxation and enabling the Government to maintain other important public expenditure priorities.

56. The Government recognises, however, that it has the responsibility of giving each industry guidance on the financial framework within which it is expected to operate. It intends, therefore, to complete as soon as possible the process of setting and publishing new financial targets after discussion with the industries. It will be the responsibility of the industries to achieve the target levels of profits set in this way and, in doing so, to reduce their costs and to continue to improve their efficiency. Each financial target will take account of any sectoral and social objectives set for that industry. These objectives will be published.

57. The following paragraphs explain how the Government intends to reintroduce and to reinforce the approach to investment appraisal, pricing policy and financial targets which was set out in the 1967 White Paper. The main theme is that, in general, if the industries do not cover the full costs of supplying goods and services efficiently, resources may be diverted from more to less worthwhile uses. By using resources in the nationalised industries, the nation foregoes their use in other parts of the economy—that is it incurs an "opportunity cost". Investment is crucial to growth; in planning their investment programmes therefore the industries should take account of the cost to the nation of the investment resources they use—the "opportunity cost of capital". The capital and other resources invested in the nationalised industries should produce a return to the nation comparable to that which they would have achieved elsewhere in the economy. Otherwise there will be a mis-allocation of resources and they will not make their full contribution to the growth of national output.

Investment and the opportunity cost of capital

58. To meet the objective that the nationalised industries should take into account the cost to the nation of the investment resources they use, the Government said in the 1967 White Paper that it expected them to appraise all important investment projects by using discounted cash flow techniques and a Test Discount Rate (T.D.R.) which, since 1969, has stood at 10% in real terms for low risk projects. It also said that pricing and output decisions should be reasonably related to long run marginal costs, including the opportunity cost of the investment resources involved.

59. A recent internal review by departments, and the N.E.D.O. report itself, have shown that the T.D.R. system has not fully lived up to expectations. In practice only a limited proportion of investment has been appraised in this way, because much of the industries' investment is regarded as part of an existing system or as necessary in terms of requirements for, say, safety standards or security of supply. This appraisal of individual projects will continue to be important, but so far the T.D.R. has neither provided nor stimulated the development of an adequate way of relating the cost of capital to the industries' financial objectives.

60. It is important for the reasons explained above that the opportunity cost of capital should be brought to bear on the industries' investment programmes as a whole, not only on some individual projects as at present. The Government is, therefore, discussing with them the development of a more direct way of relating the opportunity cost of capital to their financial performance in order to reinforce the principles of Cmnd. 3437. In this approach, which is explained in more detail in Appendix 1, the opportunity cost of capital would be represented by a required rate of return (R.R.R.) which the industries would be expected to achieve on their new investment as a whole. As such, it would become a factor in pricing policy, the scale of investment, and in the determination of financial targets.

61. The Government's judgement is that the nationalised industries should treat the opportunity cost of capital—to be earned on new investments over their working life—as 5% in real terms before tax. This judgement is based on a number of factors, set out in Appendix I, but the principal elements are the pre-tax real returns which have been achieved by private companies and the likely trend in the return on private investment. The cost of finance to the private sector has also been taken into account along with considerations of social time preference. This figure will be reviewed from time to time—normally every 3–5 years.

62. The inclusion of the opportunity cost of capital as one of the factors in determining financial targets would not mean that the targets would be set at 5% in accounting terms. The level of the target will also depend on the sectoral and social objectives which may be set for an industry and on the earning power of its existing assets. If in any case a combination of these factors pointed to any relative price adjustment, the financial target would allow for this to be phased so as to avoid sudden disruptive increases, and to take account of counter-inflation policies.

63. The financial target will remain the primary expression of the financial performance which the Government intends the industries to achieve, and development of the R.R.R. approach would not involve additional monitoring of the industries by Government.

64. Investment appraisal of individual projects will remain important. 5% is the return on investment which the Government expects the industries to achieve on their new investment as a whole, and not only on projects suitable for individual appraisal. But it will no longer specify a general T.D.R. to be used for all appraisals. The primary responsibility for operating methods of appraisal, designed to achieve 5% on new investment as a whole, will be with the industries themselves. But they will consult their sponsor departments on these methods including, for example, the choice of discount rates, and allowance for risk and for appraisal optimism. For management reasons they might choose to appraise revenue earning investments at a rate higher than 5% as a means of covering the costs of associated non-revenue investment which are also part of the cost of supply. But where investment decisions are solely concerned with the choice of the best techniques for producing a given output, or with issues concerning the phasing of capital expenditure, the appropriate discount rate would be the opportunity cost of capital rate.

65. Industries will still be required to consult their sponsoring departments on certain major investment proposals: for example, large individual projects such as power stations, steelworks, or new aerospace projects. The Government expects the industries themselves to continue to develop methods of monitoring the results of these larger projects to show that they achieve the expected returns on them.

Pricing policy

66. A major theme of the 1967 White Paper was that the nationalised industries should price to cover their long run marginal costs. The N.E.D.O. point out that for the most part they have been unable to follow this principle, not only because of price restraint and adverse market conditions but also because of serious difficulties of interpreting its practical application in particular cases. They agree that pricing policies and investment appraisal criteria should be designed to lead to the most efficient allocation of resources but stress that they should also reflect the particular market and investment environment of each nationalised industry.

67. The Government agrees that for many of the industries prices are market determined to a considerable extent and in some cases completely so. For the industries whose market position gives them scope for setting the prices they charge, the Government sees its main role as determining the overall financial target, and hence the general level of prices charged by that industry, in the light of general policy objectives, including considerations of social, sectoral and counter inflation policy, as well as the need to cover costs including the opportunity cost of capital.

68. It agrees with the N.E.D.O. that it is not sufficient for the industries to set the general level of their prices to cover their total costs. Within the overall level of prices, the industries should pay attention to the structure of prices and its relation to the structure of costs. They should ensure that, for example, charges for peak and off-peak usage are properly related to the relative costs of supply, so that the provision of capacity is properly related to the demand for it. Arbitrary cross subsidisation between different groups of consumers, which is one result of intervention in the industries' pricing policies, should be avoided. To ensure that this is happening the Government must satisfy itself that the main elements of an industry's price structure are sensibly related to the costs of supply and the market situation, and that it has developed the necessary information and accounting systems for this purpose. Subject to this, the Government believes that it is primarily for each nationalised industry to work out the details of its prices with regard to its markets and its overall objectives, including its financial target.

Financial targets

69. Financial targets are central to the guidelines which the industries expect from the Government, and they are essential for their short to medium term planning. Appendix II lists those targets which are already in force. Targets for the other industries will be set as soon as possible. Generally they will be for around 3–5 years, although a shorter period may be necessary at first for some of them.

70. A financial target must obviously be tailored to the circumstances of the particular industry. It must also be in a form which can be clearly understood and which will provide an effective discipline on the industry. The main form for the profitable industries will be a percentage return, before interest, on the average net assets employed by the industry. Alternatively, in one or two cases, a profitable industry might be set a target in terms of a percentage return on turnover—for example, if it is labour rather than capital intensive. It may also be necessary to set a short term profits target on an interim basis for Aerospace and Shipbuilders until decisions can be finalised on their longer term objectives. Those surface transport nationalised industries which require grant finance, or are running at about break even, will be set targets in terms of the amount of deficit or grant.

71. It is sometimes suggested that financial targets should be in the form of self-financing ratios. However, although forecasts of these ratios are very important in estimating the industries' requirements for Government finance, they are not a suitable basis for financial targets. Performance in relation to a target is a measure of how well an industry is using its total assets, and it is therefore necessary to relate profits earned to the total capital employed in the business rather than to the amount of its investment in a particular year. Moreover, a number of the industries have a record of shortfall on their estimates of annual investment and so a self-financing ratio target could be met or beaten for reasons in no sense attributable to efficient management. It is, nevertheless, open to the industries themselves to set targets for their own operating divisions in this, or any other form, provided that taken together these subtargets are consistent with the main published target for the industry as a whole.

72. The Government has announced that when an inflation accounting standard is approved it will apply to the nationalised industries, subject to any necessary adjustments to meet their special circumstances. It also intends that, as soon as possible, the financial targets should be put on some suitable inflation-adjusted basis. The target for telecommunications is effectively set in this way now (and some of the other industries are also already charging supplementary depreciation). The basis for the other targets will depend on the present accounting practices of the industry in question and also the timing and nature of the general move to inflation accounting.

73. The level of each financial target will be decided industry by industry. It will take account of a wide range of factors. These will include the expected return from effective, cost conscious management of existing and new assets; market prospects; the scope for improved productivity and efficiency; the opportunity cost of capital; the implications for the Public Sector Borrowing Requirement; counter-inflation policy; and social or sectoral objectives for, e.g. the energy and transport industries. When the target has been settled for the industry, the Secretary of State will announce it to Parliament. He will indicate the main assumptions on which it is based: for example, any particular social or sectoral objectives which the Government has set the industry, and which may have affected the level of the target; the broad implications for the industry's pricing; and any other important factors of which Parliament and the public should know when they subsequently judge the industry's performance against the target.

26

74. The N.E.D.O., who also recommended the re-establishment of financial targets, pointed out that there was not at present any formal procedure for nationalised industries to compare performance against target in their published accounts. They argued that this was unsatisfactory from the point of view of encouraging Parliamentary and public awareness of an industry's performance as measured by this key indicator. In practice a number of the industries have published such comparisons in the past. They have now agreed that in future all of them will show prominently in their annual reports and accounts their financial target and the outturn in terms of that target and comment on the comparison. A target often allows for variations between particular years within a period, and it will be for an industry to explain this where necessary, and also to comment on the prospects for getting back on track for the period as a whole; and on any major measures it proposes to take for this purpose.

75. In this way each nationalised industry will be given public guidance on the overall financial performance expected of it for a period of years ahead, and it will be held accountable for its performance measured by that target. For its part, the Government will be answerable for the level of target which it has agreed with the industry, and also for any subsequent intervention which may have caused the industry to deviate from its target. The Government has asked the Price Commission, when it investigates price proposals by an industry, to take account of any financial target which the Government has set and to examine to what extent the price increases proposed are necessary to achieve the target or could be reduced by cost savings.

Performance indicators

76. The N.E.D.O. propose that the guidelines to be given to the nationalised industries should include not only financial targets but also targets for other aspects of performance. They point out that by themselves financial targets do not necessarily serve the purpose of stimulating management to further efficiency, since to the extent that there is a monopoly situation the targets could be achieved by price rises or changes in the level of service.

77. The Government readily agrees that the industries' performance and efficiency cannot be measured solely in terms of whether they meet their financial targets. Much depends on how they meet them and, while they must price to cover their costs, the Government expects all the industries to continue to look for ways to improve their productivity so as to cut and control those costs. The industries will let their sponsoring department have performance indicators, including forward projections, which will provide regular and systematic information as a contribution to discussing their success in controlling costs and increasing efficiency.

78. So that the public can be better informed on the industries' success in doing this, and on their performance and service standards, the Government has decided that the published financial targets should be supplemented by publication of performance indicators. In practice the industries already publish a good deal of information but it is not always easy to see which are the most significant indicators for the particular industry. The Government has,

therefore, asked each industry, in consultation with its sponsoring department, to select a number of key performance indicators, including valid international comparisons, and to publish them prominently in their annual reports. They would be supported by an explanation of why they had been chosen and of significant trends. The indicators will vary from industry to industry and the Government recognises that some of the industries in a competitive position have to take account of requirements of commercial confidentiality. However, there will probably be some indicators common to most including, for example, labour productivity, and standards of service, where these are readily measurable. The Government has asked each industry to start publication of historic performance series as soon as they can, and preferably in their next report and accounts. There are obvious difficulties for any industry, whether nationalised or private sector, in predicting the path of all its key performance indicators in future years; and any industry has to be ready to respond to circumstances by changing priorities within its overall objectives. The Government believes, nevertheless, that the nationalised industries should be prepared to make public suitable aims in terms of performance and service, and it has asked them to do this in their reports and accounts.

Cash limits

79. The Government's White Paper on Cash Limits (Cmnd. 6440) explained that the estimates of the nationalised industries' external financing requirements, to be met by loans, Public Dividend Capital and grants, would be used as a form of cash limit. This limit applies to the current financial year only, and supplements the medium term financial target.

80. These estimates are agreed with the nationalised industries in advance. Major industries then send to their sponsoring department and to the Treasury every month—and the other industries every quarter—an up-to-date estimate of their financing requirements for the year, and their proposals for meeting them. They discuss with the departments any significant changes from the forecasts shown in the published table.

81. As Cmnd. 6440 said, these cash limits cannot be immutable. The nationalised industries recognise that this does not mean that they can normally expect an increase in their limit on account of failures of management or of developments within their own control, including responsibility for the level of their pay settlements. However, they are different from the generality of public services in that, like private sector companies, their revenues and expenditures depend on trading conditions. As a result, they may on occasion exceed their borrowing estimates for reasons beyond their own control and which do not reflect on the efficiency of their financial management; for example, a change in the forecast cash flow of an energy industry caused by an exceptional winter. But, whatever the reason, there is no presumption that if the scrutiny of the monthly financing statements shows an increase in the borrowing requirement the Government will agree to this being met by a further injection of external finance and an increase in the cash limit, as opposed to other action which the industry can take to offset a prospective increase in its financing requirements. If an increase was agreed it would be announced to Parliament by the Minister concerned.

82. The Government sees this control over financing requirements as a proper discipline on the industries' financial management, and the industries accept it as such. It allows departments to keep in close touch with developments in the industries' short-term financial position but to do so in a systematic and orderly way. The publication of the financing requirements in the form of cash limits is a useful step forward towards the objective of greater public accountability.

Capital structure and sources of finance

83. To the extent that they cannot meet their financing requirements from their own resources (profits and depreciation), the nationalised industries rely primarily on loan finance: for their medium and long term requirements, from the National Loans Fund or by foreign borrowing; and, for their short term temporary requirements, from the banks. In addition, some of them are also financed by grants; and some of them by Public Dividend Capital, on which they pay dividends to the Government.

84. The N.E.D.O. consider that the methods of financing the industries are not based on a consistent rationale. They argue that the arrangements take inadequate account of risks, that the burden of fixed interest debt can be too onerous in some cases, that the proportion of funding from reserves seems to be based on historic accident rather than principle, and that there are no convincing principles to serve as a basis for the current and future use of Public Dividend Capital.

85. The Government does not accept this criticism. It is true that the proportion of funding from reserves varies, but this results from the very varying financial circumstances and history of the industries. As explained in the following paragraphs, there are longstanding principles for Public Dividend Capital, and the Government does not accept that the majority of the nationalised industries need "risk capital". But it will introduce some greater flexibility in the arrangements for borrowing from the National Loans Fund which will be helpful to the industries.

Public Dividend Capital

86. The Government reaffirms that Public Dividend Capital will be made available only to those nationalised industries which are expected to be both fully viable and also especially subject to cyclical fluctuations in their returns as a result of their trading conditions and the nature of their assets. The nationalised industries which are now statutorily eligible to receive P.D.C., as well as loan finance, are: Airways, Steel, Giro, Aerospace and Shipbuilders (The interim basis for financing the British Steel Corporation is described in Cmnd 7149). Apart from Giro, which is in competition in the banking sector, all these industries are operating in highly competitive international markets. It is right that they should have a capital structure which does not create an annual obligation to pay an unduly large fixed amount of interest during the downturn of their trading cycle. Otherwise their published trading results could well affect their ability to win new business in their international markets. This is not to say that the issue of P.D.C. gives them a soft option. The Government would generally expect that over the period of an industry's business cycle, taking the good and bad years together, the average level of gross dividend payments would be at least as much as the interest which the Government would have received if it had advanced the money from the National Loans Fund.

87. The Government does not intend to take new statutory powers to make P.D.C. available to nationalised industries other than the five which are now eligible for issues. It is sometimes argued that nationalised industries should have P.D.C., or some form of equity finance, because a private sector company has risk capital in its balance sheet. But this argument ignores a fundamental difference between a nationalised industry and a private sector company. The latter has to arrange its borrowing so that it is not too highly geared. Its gearing ratio—the proportion of loan to share capital—will vary according to the riskiness of its activities, but if it does not have a sufficient proportion of share capital it will fail to attract further capital, share or loans. A nationalised industry in contrast looks to the Government for all its external finance which it is given either directly or with the Government's guarantee or agreement. To obtain this finance it has to satisfy the Government of the need for it, but this is done by reference to analyses of proposed investment programmes and market and financing prospects, and capital structure as such is irrelevant to the decision.

88. Some nationalised industries would in any event fail the viability test. It has always been made clear that P.D.C. is not suitable for industries which have difficulty in breaking even taking one year with another, because it would then become little more than an interest free non-repayable advance—in effect a grant. There are other industries which are financially much stronger and which no doubt could pay dividends if they had P.D.C. It is true, as N.E.D.O. point out, that these industries are not free from some degree of risk. However, it is risk of a different order from that faced by those nationalised industries which operate in international markets, and which are subject to marked cyclical variations in their trading, and from private sector companies which could in the last resort go bankrupt. The Government has, therefore, decided that those industries which are not now eligible for Public Dividend Capital will continue to be financed by loans and, in some cases, grants. The formal obligation to pay interest on loans is a discipline on these industries and, in the absence of a stimulus from the stock market to pay dividends, it is the best way of ensuring that they remunerate the finance with which the Government provides them. This is by intention a rigorous approach and if, exceptionally, it leads to a capital write-off the circumstances will be fully explained to Parliament. Where grants are made to an industry the reasons will be made public, and explained when the powers are taken and estimates laid before Parliament; and the amounts will be controlled.

Financing of the British National Oil Corporation

89. The British National Oil Corporation is in a special position with regard to financing. Government finance for the Corporation is channelled through the National Oil Account, into which all B.N.O.C.'s own revenues also flow, and which is under the direct control of the Government. B.N.O.C. therefore does not possess a conventional capital structure as such. But the Corporation operates in a highly competitive international market and the arguments in favour of flexibility set out in paragraph 86 above apply equally to it. The Government has therefore agreed with the Corporation arrangements whereby in due course 40% of its capital employed will be treated as being subject to interest, and the remainder as equivalent to equity capital on which there will be a variable return depending on the Corporation's profits and prospects.

30

Loans

90. Since 1956 the nationalised industries' medium and long term borrowing needs have been met directly by the Government, initially by issues from the Consolidated Fund and, since 1968, by loans from the National Loans Fund, except when individual industries have borrowed on the international markets. The Government has reviewed these arrangements and decided that they should continue, as providing the best means of ensuring that funds are secured for the public sector on the keenest possible terms. The reasons for this decision are explained in more detail in Appendix III, which also discusses foreign borrowing by the nationalised industries.

91. The Government has also reviewed the terms on which the industries can borrow from the N.L.F. Hitherto the rule has been that an industry should borrow for periods matched to the average lives of the classes of assets which it is financing. This ensures that the structure of its financial obligations is appropriately related to the needs and nature of its activities. It also preserves a balance between the interests of the industries and those of the general taxpayer, who has to bear the residual responsibility for the servicing of Government debt. Taken overall, the maturity pattern of new public sector debt of all kinds issued during a period is mainly determined by the interaction between the preferences of lenders for loans of particular periods and the needs of the authorities to finance the borrowing requirement in a way consistent with monetary policy. Subject to this, the monetary authorities seek to borrow in a way which minimises the total cost of borrowing by the public sector over time. It would be neither practicable nor consistent with this approach to vary the maturity pattern of borrowing by the N.L.F. to match the preferences of individual public sector bodies to which it on lent. As a result, if the nationalised industries were free to choose the borrowing terms from the N.L.F. most favourable to them (for example, borrowing short when they expected rates to fall and long when they expected them to rise) they would be minimising their contribution to the servicing of Government debt, without changing the total debt servicing cost of the Government: their saving would be at the expense of the general taxpayer who bears the residual costs. Nevertheless, the Government recognises that these arrangements may have led to a situation in which some industries have a debt structure with temporary and long term debt but little or no medium term. To meet this point, while still preserving the main features of the present criteria, the industries will in future be allowed to borrow, if they wish, for medium term maturities up to 20% of their N.L.F. borrowing which they would otherwise borrow long term.

92. The Government is also prepared to consider in suitable cases proposals for the capitalisation in an industry's accounts of the interest charge over a period (that is, the interest paid on loans to finance specific capital expenditure projects is treated as part of the cost of those projects and written off over their life rather than, as is usual practice, charged to revenue in the year in which the interest liability accrues). Capitalisation can be appropriate when an industry is financing a major expansion of its capital assets and the new investment will not yield revenue during a long construction period, and the practice is already adopted for certain capital intensive industries. But such cases are rare, and in every one the Government must first satisfy itself that the procedure

31

is fully justified, and consistently applied by the industry, and that the future revenues flowing from the asset will be sufficient to cover the total costs including the capitalised interest.

CONCLUSION

93. The N.E.D.O. concluded that the evidence which they had accumulated pointed overwhelmingly to the need to base the nationalised industries' relationship with government on trust, continuity and accountability. These three concepts cannot be guaranteed by legislation, by new machinery of control or indeed by principles and objectives discussed in a White Paper. Nevertheless, the Government accepts them as aims to be achieved, and it believes that the measures and approach now proposed will produce a lasting improvement in its relations with the industries. It hopes that Parliament, and the Select Committee on Nationalised Industries, will find that the proposals—and particularly those for improved accountability—will provide a better basis for their continuing scrutiny of the nationalised industries and of the departments which deal with them.

THE REQUIRED RATE OF RETURN ON INVESTMENT (R.R.R.)

1. Paragraph 60 says that the Government is discussing with the industries the development of a more direct way of relating the opportunity cost of capital to their financial performance. This Appendix sets out the main principles of the R.R.R. approach. Discussions between departments and the nationalised industries on its implementation will continue.

Objectives

2. The R.R.R. approach is directed at the efficient allocation of resources, although in pursuit of this aim it has to fit in with other policies which may be laid down for the nationalised industries. It is a development of the principles set out in Cmnd. 3437 (Nationalised Industries: A Review of Economic and Financial Objectives) for ensuring that the cost to the nation of the resources used by the industries is adequately reflected in the industries' investment and pricing policies. Cmnd. 3437 required the setting of financial objectives, which would flow from consideration of appropriate investment and pricing policies, and the Government intends that this should continue but in a more practical way. However, the return on investment is only one factor to be taken into account. Social, sectoral and wider economic considerations will continue to influence the Government's determination of financial objectives.

3. The objective of the R.R.R. is to remedy two deficiencies in present practice (see paragraph 59 of the main paper). First, it is designed to bring the opportunity cost of capital into the determination of an industry's investment programme as a whole and not just into the appraisal of individual projects; secondly, it aims to include the opportunity cost of capital more directly in the determination of the industries' financial targets.

Method of application and relevance to pricing and investment decisions

4. The R.R.R. approach would operate by incorporating the opportunity cost of capital into the cost of supplying increments of output. The cost of capital would be represented by a d.c.f. rate of return (the R.R.R.) which investments should yield over their working lives. When applied to the investment programme as a whole, including items which are not regarded as revenue earning investment but which are costs none the less, it would determine the capital element in marginal costs.

5. The method of applying this capital cost el ement in the circumstances of individual industries would depend very much on the information available. Where an industry already makes estimates of its long run marginal costs these could be applied directly, using the 5% R.R.R. to calculate the capital element. In other cases, more approximate estimates may need to be used, for example, by taking the investment programme, relating it to the output associated with that investment and estimating the price at which this output would have to sell in order to cover all the costs, including capital costs, involved in producing it. Discussions with the industries have indicated various ways in which this might be done.

6. Thus it would be possible to make an estimate of the costs associated with the output resulting from the proposed investment programmes: in other words, an operational estimate of marginal costs. In public utility industries, which have some scope for setting their own prices, the cost of capital, represented by the R.R.R., would enter directly into pricing policy and through market demand into determining future output. In industries which have to accept prices set by the markets in which they operate, revenue estimates would be based on assumptions about future market

prices. The R.R.R. approach would provide a measure of costs to be compared with these prices, and hence a test of the economic viability of the investment programme as a whole.

7. It would not be appropriate to apply the R.R.R. to a major business sector where social obligations imply continuing losses which the Government has agreed to cover by payment of deficit grant. But in the case of grant support provided for isolated services where, for the most part, costs are covered by revenue from users, it might be convenient to count grant as part of the general stream of revenue justifying investment.

Relation to financial targets

8. The R.R.R. is not the same as the financial target for an industry, although it is an element in its determination. There are two main practical problems. First, because financial targets will be expressed in accounting terms, the R.R.R. must be translated into such terms. Second, because investment planning and financial targets work on different time scales, the financial target can only be based on a slice of the longer term cost and revenue picture.

i) Translation into accounting terms

9. This translation is inevitably indirect. The general method is to take the revenue requirement, estimated by the methods referred to in paragraphs 4 and 5, and convert this into a revenue requirement for the industry as a whole. In the case of industries where the outputs of old and new assets are indistinguishable, total revenue would be derived directly from the price needed to earn the R.R.R. on new investment; where the price which can be charged for the output of old assets is different from that which would be charged for that of new assets, it will be necessary to take account of this in deriving the total revenue figure. Costs, including depreciation, would then be deducted and the resultant net profit would be expressed as a return either on assets* (as valued according to the accounting policies of the day) or some other appropriate base. Changes in an industry's accounting policies, e.g. in calculating depreciation or valuing assets, would not necessitate any changes in prices or outputs.

ii) Relationship of different time scales

10. Whereas the R.R.R. would be applied to new investment which might have very long lead times, the period to which an industry's financial target would apply would be much shorter. If the industry was operating in stable conditions and without major discontinuities, there would be a reasonably stable relationship between the R.R.R. and the financial target, but this may not apply in other cases where investment characteristically takes the form of large and irregular projects, or where very long term and major restructuring was in progress. Nevertheless, even in these circumstances the systematic application of a standardised approach to the costs and revenue streams associated with proposed investment would help in making strategic decisions on it.

Practical application

11. The calculations involved in the R.R.R. approach would need to be made as and when financial targets were determined, or varied. The R.R.R. calculations would be the responsibility of the industries and the links between investment and financial performance should arise out of the Corporate Plan. They would be an element in the discussions leading up to the determination of the financial target.

---

*A figure derived in this way from a common 5% R.R.R. would not necessarily be the same for all industries, or even very close to 5%. First, the R.R.R. relates to the earnings of new investment over its working life, whereas the financial target would relate to the earnings on all assets over a period of, say, 3 years. Secondly, the R.R.R. is a real terms d.c.f. rate and as such is independent of accounting conventions such as the treatment of depreciation or the valuation of assets.

12. The importance of the opportunity cost of capital would vary with the capital intensity of the individual industries. But it would be only one of the many factors relevant to determining the published financial target by which the industries' financial performance over the period of the target would be measured and monitored. Moreover, the level of financial targets will not depend simply on considerations of resource allocation, but also on the weight given to social, sectoral, and wider economic policies such as the need to counter inflation.

Determination of the R.R.R. number

13. If resources are used for investment by the nationalised industries, the nation forgoes their use in other parts of the economy—i.e. it incurs an opportunity cost. It should, therefore, seek to ensure that these resources achieve a return comparable to the benefits which they would have yielded elsewhere. But there can be no unique measure of this opportunity cost: we cannot, for instance, say precisely how the resources would otherwise have been used, e.g. for private investment or for consumption. It is, therefore, necessary to look at the most relevant evidence bearing in mind problems of measurement, and to make a judgement.

14. The T.D.R. was set in 1967 at 8% as being "broadly consistent . . . with the average [pre-tax] rate of return in real terms looked for on low-risk projects in the private sector . . .". It was raised to 10% in 1969 partly in response to evidence about the appraisal rates used in the private sector and partly because of the pressure on resources following sterling devaluation in 1967. But as the focus of the R.R.R. is on the return yielded by investment as a whole rather than on the expected return on individual projects, it is appropriate to emphasise, as far as private sector profitability is concerned, the evidence on the achieved return on their total investment.

15. The main piece of evidence used to determine the R.R.R., albeit modified by less tangible factors, was a projection of the pre-tax real rate of return on assets achieved by private companies in recent years*. As the chart shows, the rate for industrial and commercial companies has fallen from over 10% in the mid-sixties to around 8% in the early seventies. In the last three years it has been very low (around 4%), but the profit rate achieved in the deepest recession since the thirties is not the best guide to prospective profits in the next 5-10 years. It is important to form a realistic view about prospective profitability in setting a required rate of return on nationalised industry investment. But exactly what rate should be postulated for the medium term future must be a matter of judgement. On the one hand, there has been a downward trend in profitability; real returns have fallen at a rate of about one percentage point every three years since the T.D.R. was set at 8% in 1967. On the other hand, while profitability will undoubtedly improve as the economy recovers from the recession, the likelihood of continued slow growth in the world economy will mean that private sector profitability, outside the North Sea sector, is unlikely to rise very rapidly for some years ahead; meanwhile, the longer term decline may well continue.

16. The cost of external capital to private firms is another relevant factor; this has the advantage of being a forward looking measure. There are, however, considerable problems of measurement and interpretation. The measure developed by the Bank of England† has varied between 7% and 12% before tax during the 1960s and early 1970s and is currently estimated to be about 7%; but although the cost of capital declined somewhat during the 1960s along with rates of return, the trend since then is not clear. In recent years, however, this measure has been affected by the extreme uncertainties of financial markets and may not therefore be a reliable guide to more settled conditions.

---

*It is recognised that accounting ratios are an imperfect basis for deriving a d.c.f. rate of return, but there is no evidence on achieved d.c.f. returns. A pre-tax rate is relevant because tax payments are part of the return to the nation on investment in the private sector.

†Quarterly Bulletin, June 1976 and June 1977.

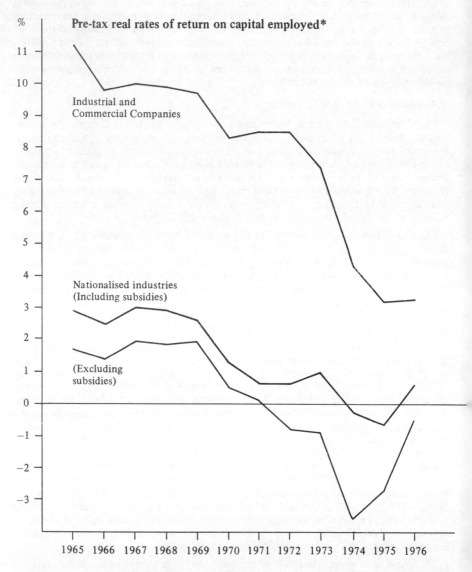

%

Pre-tax real rates of return on capital employed*

Industrial and
Commercial Companies

Nationalised industries
(Including subsidies)

(Excluding
subsidies)

1965 1966 1967 1968 1969 1970 1971 1972 1973 1974 1975 1976

* Defined as gross trading profits (or surpluses) plus rent received less capital consumption at replacement cost and less stock appreciation as a percentage of net capital stock at replacement cost plus book value of stocks. The estimates are based on national accounts data. The figures for industrial and commercial companies were published in an article 'Companies' rate of return on capital employed 1960 to 1976' in Trade and Industry for 16 September 1977

17. Many economists favour a public sector discount rate based on a measure of social time preference (S.T.P.) rather than on considerations of private sector profitability. This would point to a required rate of return based on S.T.P. But it would not provide a firm basis because of extreme difficulties of measurement. None of the methods of measuring S.T.P. is satisfactory, but what methods have been used produce figures which, given the downward trend in profitability and the difficulties of estimation, may not be significantly different from prospective profit rates.

18. The exact choice of a figure for the R.R.R. must be a matter of judgement in the light of the evidence reviewed above; there is no unique "theoretically correct" basis. However, for the reasons given in paragraph 14, the evidence on private sector appraisal rates is of little relevance. The notion of social time preference does not of itself provide an adequate basis, although in normal circumstances it would suggest choosing a number somewhat below that implied by the rate of profit. It is more important to take a hard look at the prospective profitability of investment. Hence a considerable weight must be given to evidence on the private sector rates of return actually achieved in the past and (subject to measurement problems, which have recently been very acute) to the cost of external capital. Private sector rates of return, allowing for cyclical variations, have shown a declining trend. But the level of the last few years (about 4%) is very low indeed, and it would be right to allow for some recovery from this depressed level.

19. For these reasons, the Government has decided that 5% pre-tax in real terms (i.e. after allowing for inflation) is the appropriate figure, in current circumstances, to use as a required rate of return on investment for nationalised industries. It is this rate, rather than the rate of interest of loans (usually lower in real terms), which represents the cost of capital to the nation and which should therefore influence decisions on investment and pricing.

FINANCIAL TARGETS

1. The following financial targets have been published:

British Airways ... ... 11% average rate of return on mean net assets, 1975–76 to 1978–79.

British Transport Docks Board 20% at least on mean net assets by 1980.

Telecommunications ... ... 6% a year on mean net assets revalued to replacement cost, from 1976–77 to 1978–79 (see note (ii)).

Posts ... ... 2% return on turnover for each of the financial years 1978–79 and 1979–80 (see note (iii)).

Giro ... ... 12½% annual average return on Public Dividend Capital plus retained profits over the period 1975–76 to 1977–78 (see note (iv)).

Notes:

(i) With the exception of Posts and Giro the above target returns are set after depreciation but before interest on medium and long term borrowing. They are set before interest to show how the industry has managed its resources, irrespective of the way it is financed. The returns should be sufficient, nevertheless, to cover annual interest charges (and dividends where appropriate).

(ii) This target is in real terms, i.e. after historic and supplementary depreciation and with the net assets base revalued from historic to replacement costs. All other targets are in terms of historic costs.

(iii) The Posts return is after historic and supplementary depreciation and after charging interest.

(iv) The Giro return is after interest on the N.L.F. debt remaining following the 1975 capital reconstruction.

2. The position on the other surface transport industries is as follows. All of them have the statutory duty to break even. In the case of *British Railways* break even is to be achieved after receipt of grants, predetermined on a reducing scale, towards the costs of the railway passenger business, and, up to the end of 1977, central government grants covering the deficit on the rail freight and parcels business. *British Waterways* are to break even after receipt of support grants from government; the *National Bus Company* and the *Scottish Transport Group* are to do so after receipt of revenue support grants from local authorities. Through the Public Expenditure Survey, British Railways, British Waterways and the shipping services of the Scottish Transport Group have been set the task of managing their business so that the level of central government support does not rise in real terms during the Survey period. The *National Freight Corporation* is in receipt of cash flow deficit grant pending a capital reconstruction.

3. Financial targets for the other nationalised industries will be set as soon as possible.

BORROWING ARRANGEMENTS

1. Since 1956 the nationalised industries' medium and long term borrowing needs have been met directly by the Government, except in so far as they have borrowed on the international markets. As stated in paragraph 90 of the main paper, the Government has decided that these arrangements should continue, though with greater flexibility in the terms of borrowing from the N.L.F. This Appendix explains the reasons for this decision, and also the main features of the present arrangements. There is no change in the present arrangements for short term borrowing whereby the industries borrow for periods of less than one year from the market.

Borrowing from the National Loans Fund

2. The experience in the 1950's was that, although nationalised industries' stocks were traded in virtually as if they were Government stocks, the period for which the industries could borrow, even when the issue was underwritten by the Issue Department of the Bank of England (in effect an extension of the central government), was generally shorter than that for which the Government could borrow; and that the yield offered on nationalised industry issues had to be a little higher. The higher yield was required essentially because the smaller size of the issues reduced their future marketability. Even though the timing of the issues was controlled by the Bank of England in relation to market conditions, the Bank was all too often left to take up the larger part of issues, which it then had to sell as it does Government tap stocks. The decision was therefore taken to simplify the position and make use directly of the Government's ability to secure the keenest terms on new issues. Thus under present arrangements the Treasury does the market borrowing and advances loans as necessary via the N.L.F.

3. The Government considers that to revert to the pre-1956 arrangements of allowing the industries direct access to the markets for borrowing other than short term would bring serious disadvantages. The experience in the 1950's supports the judgement that they would generally have to pay a fraction more than would the Government for borrowing for a comparable period. Thus there would be an increase in the costs of servicing the public sector debt as a whole. Moreover, because the industries would be borrowing with the Government's guarantee, explicit or implicit, they would not attract new risk capital but funds already destined to be placed in public sector debt; and so whatever the period for which they borrowed they would replace a corresponding amount of central government borrowing from that section of the market. This change in the distribution of the burden of public sector debt service would be to the disadvantage of the general taxpayer who, as explained in paragraph 91, bears the residual costs.

4. In addition to these increased costs, there would be further disadvantages in market borrowing. If the industries borrowed in the form of stock issues this would complicate the management of the gilt-edged market; and do so at a time when it is very desirable that the Government should finance as much as possible of the Public Sector Borrowing Requirement from outside the banking system. The adoption of targets for the monetary aggregates has reinforced the importance of this. If industries borrowed by way of medium term loans from the banks this might in the future affect the capacity of the banking system to provide medium term finance for exports and for private industry generally. This is not a constraint at present, but the clearing banks have expressed to Sir Harold Wilson's Committee, which is reviewing financial institutions, concern that prudential considerations might at some stage limit their capacity to provide medium term credit. It seems desirable on industrial policy grounds to avoid the risk of this particular form of crowding out by the public sector.

5. The interest which the industries pay on their N.L.F. loans is determined by Section 5 of the National Loans Act 1968. This provides for the rate of interest to be not less than that at which the Treasury are, for the time being, able to borrow for a comparable period and on other comparable terms. It is the practice for such loans to be made at rates directly linked to the current yield on Government securities. Borrowing from the N.L.F. does give nationalised industries one form of flexibility which they could not always secure if they borrowed from the market. The Government will accept premature repayment of the loans which it makes to nationalised industries, subject to an appropriate premium or discount to allow for any changes in interest rates, but not subject to any penalty. Such a facility for premature repayment would not be available to a nationalised industry if it borrowed by means of a stock issue, nor would it necessarily be available if it borrowed medium term from a bank.

Foreign Borrowing

6. It is also possible for the nationalised industries to meet a part of their requirements by borrowing overseas. However, any decisions about this must be taken in the broader context of the U.K.'s official external financing needs for the balance of payments, and the Government therefore maintains control over the amount and timing of such borrowing.

7. In recent years, there has been substantial borrowing overseas by the nationalised industries, and this has played an important role in helping to meet both the borrowing requirements of the nationalised industries themselves, and the overall financing needs of the balance of payments. But, with rapidly improving prospects on the current account of the balance of payments, and a much improved level of official reserves, the situation has changed considerably. The scope for foreign borrowing by the nationalised industries over the next few years will reflect these changed circumstances.

8. Most foreign borrowing by nationalised industries is undertaken with a Treasury guarantee. The Bank of England provide advice about borrowing opportunities in the international markets and operate an informal queue whereby prospective nationalised industry borrowers can be brought to the market in an orderly manner as and when suitable borrowing opportunities arise. The nationalised industries generally can also borrow from the European Investment Bank and, in addition, the British Steel Corporation and the National Coal Board are eligible for European Coal and Steel Community loans.

9. In addition, industries borrowing foreign currency can choose to do so under the Exchange Cover Scheme operated under the powers of the Exchange Equalisation Account. This Scheme relieves them of any exchange risk associated with foreign currency borrowing. In return, the E.E.A. retains a part of the interest differential between the rate on the foreign currency loan and the appropriate N.L.F. rate: the net effect is to reduce the cost of borrowing to the industry by a margin of about 1% below the rate it would normally pay to the N.L.F.

10. The financial effect within the U.K. of foreign borrowing by the industries is very much the same as that of their N.L.F. borrowing. This is particularly so in the case of borrowing under the Exchange Cover Scheme where the foreign currency proceeds are sold as soon as they are received by the industries to the Exchange Equalisation Account, which makes sterling available in return, and which itself in turn has to be financed by central government borrowing through sales of gilt edged securities or Treasury Bills.

11. Two special points apply to the British National Oil Corporation and British Airways.   B.N.O.C. can raise finance without Government guarantee because it deals in an internationally traded commodity which is customarily priced in dollars.   British Airways also has opportunities for foreign borrowing on overseas markets not open to the rest of the public sector in view of their special requirements for overseas finance.

Printed in England for Her Majesty's Stationery Office by Oyez Press Limited
Dd291735   K80   3/78

HER MAJESTY'S STATIONERY OFFICE

Government Bookshops

49 High Holborn, London WC1V 6HB
13a Castle Street, Edinburgh EH2 3AR
41 The Hayes, Cardiff CF1 1JW
Brazennose Street, Manchester M60 8AS
Southey House, Wine Street, Bristol BS1 2BQ
258 Broad Street, Birmingham B1 2HE
80 Chichester Street, Belfast BT1 4JY

*Government publications are also available
through booksellers*

ISBN 0 10 171310 X